From Spain to America

by Ellen B. Cutler

PEARSON

Scott
Foresman

Editorial Offices: Glenview, Illinois • Parsippany, New Jersey • New York, New York
Sales Offices: Needham, Massachusetts • Duluth, Georgia • Glenview, Illinois
Coppell, Texas • Ontario, California • Mesa, Arizona

ISBN: 0-328-13422-8

8 9 10 V0G1 14 13 12 11 10 09 08

From Spain

Have you ever thought about the word *rodeo*? It's from the Spanish word *rodear,* which means "to surround." *Rodeo* is also a Spanish word meaning "the job of rounding up cattle." It has the same meaning in English.

Many words that we use in English have been borrowed from Spanish. This borrowing happens when people who speak different languages mix together. Over time the languages mix and mingle too! The mixing started when Christopher Columbus sailed with a fleet of three ships from his home in Spain in 1492.

Niña, Pinta, and Santa Maria

3

Columbus says good-bye.

The Explorers

Columbus and his crew set sail in search of *oro,* the Spanish word for gold. They hoped to land in Asia, where they could fill their pockets with gold and other riches. Columbus believed he could reach Asia by sailing due west from Spain. His crew did not believe him. The men were angry and scared. They may have **shrieked** in fear, not knowing what lay ahead. His crew's distrust **offended** Columbus, but he still felt confident.

Columbus and his men found islands dotted with small villages. Today this place is called the Bahamas. The people there led simple lives. They fished in the ocean. They ate food that seemed strange to the Spanish men—sweet potatoes, corn, peanuts, and pineapples. They carved tools and toys out of bone, shell, stone, and wood. Columbus was sure these people were natives of India. So he called them "Indians."

Columbus finds land.

A Spanish conquistador

Some of the Indians wore armbands and necklaces made out of pure gold. Columbus was sure he had found Asia.

Columbus was wrong.

No maps marked this land and no books described it, but Columbus had landed here. Other explorers were on the way. Spanish military leaders, or conquistadors, were following Columbus and his men.

The conquistadors came with large armies. They cut through jungles, crossed deserts, and climbed mountains. They set out to explore and conquer the New World. They also hoped they would find gold.

Conquistador helmet

Mission San Jose, San Antonio, Texas

Other Influences

The conquistadors fought and conquered new lands for Spain. But they were not the only people who came to the New World. Missionaries, or religious people, came to spread their customs and beliefs in the New World. The missionaries built missions, or churches, that reflected their Spanish culture and building traditions.

Soon Spanish became the language that was spoken the most in the New World. American gold and other goods brought wealth to Spain for more than three hundred years. Spain also did America **favors** by bringing over horses. Some of these horses escaped to roam free. Now, these American horses are called *mustangs,* from the Spanish word meaning "an ownerless animal." Spanish also gave a word to mustangs that were too wild to ride: *bronco.* Cowboys **lassoed** these wild horses and trained them. Mustangs were then a part of the legend of the American West.

Horses running in the West

Spanish and English Words

Many other Spanish words crept into the English language. You may have noticed that many words you know in English are similar to or the same as the words in Spanish. Did you know that the word *alligator* comes from the Spanish word *el lagarto,* "the lizard"? In Spanish, *fiesta* can mean "celebration" or "feast." We use the word *fiesta* to mean a party in English too. *Lasso,* a cowboy's rope, comes from Spanish. So does *hacienda,* "a large farm," and *ranch,* "a small farm."

Spanish: *el lagarto*

English: *alligator*

Spanish: *fiesta*

English: *fiesta*

Did you know that the word *cargo* also comes from Spanish? In Spanish, the verb *cargar* means "to load." So it would make sense that *cargo* is often *loaded* onto ships, trains, and trucks to be sent out. The word *cockroach* may have been formed because this English word sounds like the Spanish name *cucaracha*.

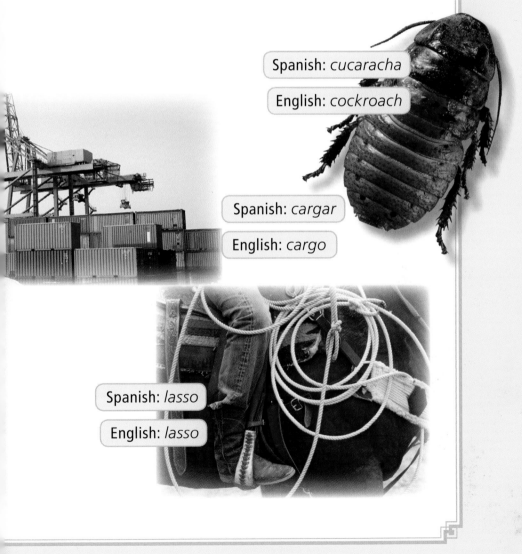

Spanish: *cucaracha*

English: *cockroach*

Spanish: *cargar*

English: *cargo*

Spanish: *lasso*

English: *lasso*

Map of Texas and
its surrounding areas

San Antonio

Spanish explorers came to the area near San Antonio, Texas, in 1691. They arrived on the feast day of Saint Anthony of Padua. They named the place in honor of the saint.

The city of San Antonio shares its name with the river that runs through it. The first settlements along the San Antonio River were missions. It is easy to see the Spanish influence in these southwestern towns.

Most of the area was open **prairie** when settlers first arrived. Forests covered the hills in the east. Trees filled the canyons and riverbanks. Herds of deer and bison roamed across the plains. Wildflowers of blue, pink, red, and yellow dotted the tall green grass.

The explorers claimed the land for Spain. There was plenty of fresh water and trees for wood. The countryside had good hunting.

Wildlife and waterfalls on the San Antonio Missions Trail

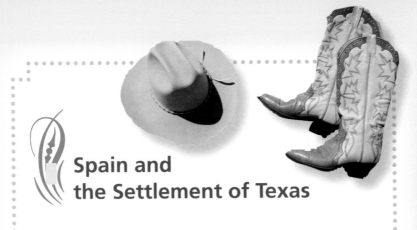

Spain and the Settlement of Texas

October 12, 1492: Christopher Columbus comes ashore in the eastern Bahamas.

1512: Missions begin to be built throughout Spanish territories.

1520s: Spanish explorers first sail in the Gulf of Mexico along the Texas coast.

1691: Texas is a separate Spanish region; explorers name the San Antonio River.

1718: Mission San Antonio de Valero and San Antonio de Bejar are built.

1731: Fifteen Spanish families arrive to settle in San Antonio.

1821: Mexico, which includes Texas, declares its independence from Spain.

1845: Texas becomes the 28th U.S. state.

In 1718 the mission of San Antonio de Valero was built next to the San Antonio de Bejar military post.

San Antonio did not become a proper town for another thirteen years. In 1731 fifteen families finally arrived from Spain to make their homes in this new world. The trip had been long and hard. Many people died along the way.

Their new homes were a **bargain.** They could live in the comfort and safety of the military post while building houses. The land cost nothing. It was rich and beautiful. They could imagine fields full of crops along both sides of the **riverbed.**

Difficult Times

For about fifty years the settlers and missions in San Antonio enjoyed peace and good times. American Indians and Spanish settlers got along well. Troops provided protection against any kind of attack. However, life became more dangerous and difficult for the American Indians toward the end of the eighteenth century.

Life along the
San Antonio River

American Indian men, women, and children

Illnesses that had little effect on Europeans were deadly to many American Indians. Their numbers grew smaller and smaller due to these illnesses as well as battles. With fewer people to educate, the missions became less important. The beautiful mission churches in San Antonio now fell into disrepair.

By 1821 Spain had lost most of its lands in America. Along with losing the lands, the missions were taken away from the religious Spanish groups. Beautiful buildings with rich architecture like San Antonio de Valero (now known as the Alamo) were made into government buildings or turned over to private businesses. Texas became the twenty-eighth state of the United States of America in 1845.

Texas Flag

The riverwalk in San Antonio

Beautiful San Antonio

Today, the missions along the San Antonio River remind people of the old Spanish culture. New buildings and busy people make San Antonio an exciting city.

We have seen how language blends the old with the new. Our American culture is a colorful mixture of unique people from many different backgrounds, customs, and traditions. Together, Spanish San Antonio and modern San Antonio create a truly American culture.

Glossary

bargain *n.* an agreement to trade or exchange; deal.

favors *n.* acts of kindness; gifts.

lassoed *v.* caught with a long rope with a loop on one end.

offended *v.* hurt the feelings of someone; made angry; displeased; pained.

prairie *n.* a large area of level or rolling land with grass but few or no trees.

riverbed *n.* a channel in which a river flows or used to flow.

shrieked *v.* made a loud, sharp, shrill sound.